UA

FUN
WITH
MAGNETS

Ed Catherall

Science is Fun

Balls and Balloons	**Growing Plants**
Clay Play	**Light and Dark**
Colours	**Mirrors and Lenses**
Floating and Sinking	**Our Pets**
Fun with Magnets	**Sand Play**
Fun with Wheels	**Wind Play**

Illustrations by George Fryer

First published in 1985 by
Wayland (Publishers) Ltd
61 Western Road, Hove
East Sussex BN3 1JD, England

British Library Cataloguing in Publication Data
Catherall, Ed
Fun with magnets. – (Science is fun)
1. Magnets – Juvenile literature
I. Title   II. Series
538′.2   QC757.5

ISBN 0–85078–690–8

Phototypeset by
Kalligraphics Ltd, Redhill, Surrey
Printed in Italy by
G. Canale & C.S.p.A., Turin
Bound in the U.K. by
The Bath Press, Avon

CONTENTS

Care of your magnets

Collect many different magnets.
What shapes are your magnets?
Draw these different magnet shapes.

Which of your magnets have 'keepers'?
Replace the keepers when you store your magnets.
Never store your magnets close together.

Attraction

Take a strong magnet, a pen and
a pad of paper.

Make a list of things which your magnet attracts.
What are these things made of?
Make a list of things your magnet does not attract.
What are these things made of?
What do you notice?

Magnets and metals

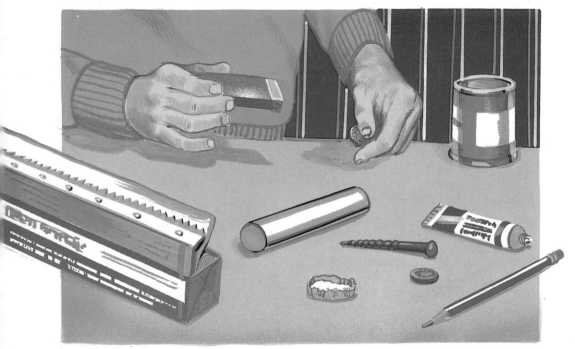

Collect many small metal objects.
Collect objects such as steel nails, brass screws,
copper piping and different coins.

Which metals does your magnet attract?

Which metals are not attracted to your magnet?

A magnetic holder

Feel the magnetic power when your magnet
attracts a large object.
Try the refrigerator door.
Does your magnet stick to this object?

Put a sheet of paper on the refrigerator door.
Does your magnet hold the paper to the door?
You have made a magnetic holder.

Magnetic power

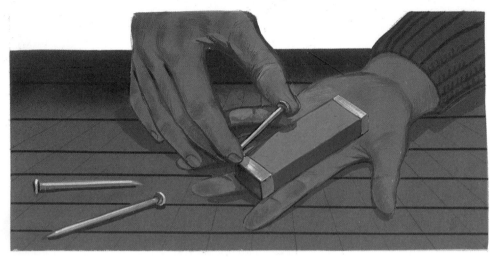

Which part of a magnet do you use to attract things?
Put a small nail on the end of your magnet.
Pull the nail.
Can you feel the magnetic power?

Put the nail in the middle of your magnet.
What do you feel when you pull the nail?

How many tacks can you hang from
one end of your magnet?
How many tacks can you hang from the middle?

Magnetic fishing

Cut some fish shapes out of paper.
Attach a paper-clip to each fish.
Write different numbers on each fish.
Put the fish in a box.

Fix a length of thread to a magnet.
Tie the other end of the thread to a stick.

Use your magnet to catch paper fish.
Add up the numbers on the fish you catch.
The person with the highest total is the winner.

Magnets and glass

Put a tack in an empty glass jar.
Can you move the tack up the inside of the jar by
moving your magnet up the outside of the jar?
Does your magnet attract through glass?

Does your magnet attract through a china cup?
Does your magnet attract through a plastic cup?

10

Magnets and water

Put a tack in a jar full of water.
Hold your magnet over the water.
Does the tack rise through the water?
Does your magnet attract through water?

Put your magnet in the water.
Does your magnet work under water?

Use a cloth to dry your magnet before storing it.

A wrapped magnet

Wrap your magnet in a cotton cloth.
Does your wrapped magnet attract
a tack through the cotton?

Does your magnet attract through nylon or wool?
Does your magnet attract through
a rubber balloon?
Does your magnet attract when wrapped
in metal foil?

Steering a ball bearing

Find a strong sheet of cardboard.
Use books to hold the cardboard above the table.
Put a steel ball bearing on the cardboard.

Hold a magnet under the cardboard.
Pull the ball along with the magnet.

Draw a racetrack on the cardboard.
Use your magnet to steer the ball along the track.

Playing with magnets

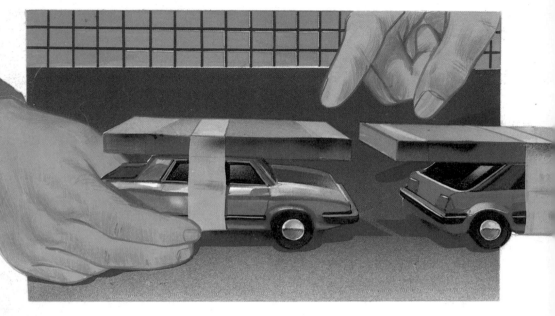

Find two strong bar magnets.
Find two small toy cars shorter than the magnets.
Use sticky tape to fix a magnet to each car.

Place the cars so that the magnets are attracted.
Can one car tow the other?

Place the cars so that the magnets push them apart.
Notice how the magnets repel each other.

14

Pictures with magnets

Put iron filings into an empty salt-shaker.
Draw a face on a sheet of cardboard.
Sprinkle iron filings on to the cardboard.

Hold a magnet under the cardboard.
Move the iron filings to give the face
hair and a beard.

Draw other pictures for your iron filings.

Patterns with magnets

Put a magnet between two books.
Place a sheet of cardboard or clear plastic.
over the books.
Sprinkle iron filings from
a salt-shaker on to the cardboard.
Gently tap the cardboard.
What patterns do the iron filings make?
What happens if you put two magnets
under the cardboard?

16

A nail and a magnet

Try to pick up a tack with a large steel nail.

Touch the head of your nail with a magnet.
Now does the nail pick up the tack?
Slowly remove the magnet from the nail.
What happens?

What happens if you use a brass nail or
a wooden stick?

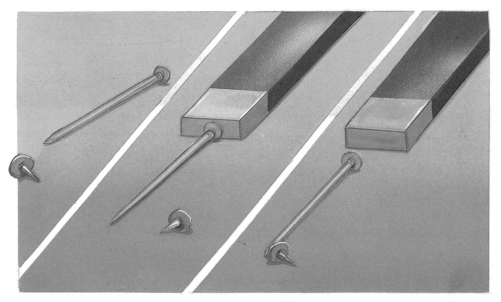

Making your own magnet

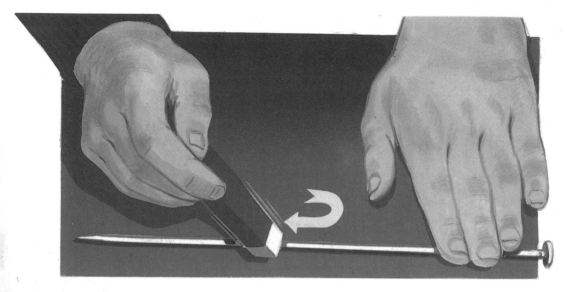

Put a long steel nail on a table.
Hold it still with your finger.
Stroke the nail twenty times with
one end of a magnet.

Always stroke the nail in the same direction.
Always use the same end of the magnet.

Try to pick up a tack with the nail.
Have you made the nail into a magnet?

Banging a magnet

Make a magnet from a large steel nail (see page 18).
How many tacks can you hang from
one end of the nail?

Bang the nail twenty times on the edge of the table.

Now how many tacks can you hang
from the end of the nail?
What does banging the nail magnet do?

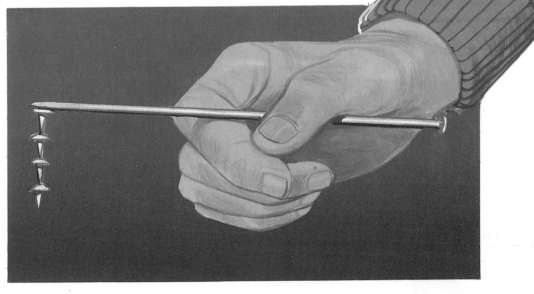

A magnetic boat

Make a magnet from a steel needle (see page 18).
Push the needle through the top of a cork.
Push a tack into the bottom of the cork.
Your tack acts as a keel to your boat.

Float your cork boat on water in a large bowl.
Use a magnet to steer your magnetic boat.
What do you notice about your needle magnet?

Making a compass

Use a cork to make a magnetic boat (see page 20).
Float your cork boat on water in a large bowl.
Which way does the needle magnet point?

Move your needle boat.
What happens?
Now which way does the needle magnet point?

North and south poles

Make a sticky-tape sling to hold a bar magnet.
Place the magnet in the sling.

Make a hole near each end of the tape.
Fix thread through the holes.

Hold your magnet up by the thread.
Notice that one end of the magnet points north.
This is the 'north-seeking pole' of the magnet.
The other end is the 'south-seeking pole'.

Magnetic toys

Look for magnets in toys.
Notice how the magnets are used.

Which toys use the magnetic power to attract?
Which toys use the magnetic power to repel?

Have you any games that use magnetic power?
Look for other places where magnets are used.

GLOSSARY

Attract   To make something come nearer.

Compass   An instrument that always shows you where north is. A compass can help you find your way when you are lost.

Iron filings   Tiny pieces of iron.

Keel   A long piece of wood or metal fixed to the bottom of a boat to help it stay upright.

Keeper   A small iron bar placed across the end of a magnet to stop it losing its magnetic power.

Magnetic poles   The two ends of a magnet.

Repel   To force an object away.

Steer   To make an object move in the direction you want.

INDEX